the passive income millionaire

Earn More. Live Without Compromise.

Matt Voss

DISTRICT HOUSE

DOWNLOAD YOUR FREE GIFT!

As a thank-you for buying this book, I'd like to offer you the free **Passive Income Millionaire Cheat Sheet**. You can use this cheat sheet as a "quick and dirty" summary of all the passive income ideas and strategies covered in this book. Compare the pros and cons of various alternative income methods, and determine which ones are right for you. Download the cheat sheet right now by visiting my website, or scan the QR code below:

https://districthousepublishing.com/passive

SCAN ME

Contents

Introduction

Consider this:

Would you rather have $1,000,000, or a penny that doubles in value every day for thirty days?

The classic thought experiment offers us a nice introduction to the topic of this book. Go ahead and take just a moment to decide:

You're on a stroll one day and spot a penny on the sidewalk. When you stoop down to pick it up, you learn that this is no ordinary penny, but a magical coin that doubles in value every day. In other words, on day two you would have two pennies, on day three four pennies, eight pennies on day four, and so on. It's a neat trick, you admit, but perhaps you'd give it away without a moment's thought to a shrewd businessman who comes up and offers you one million dollars for it. Later, upon learning the *power of compounding*, you realize you've made a terrible mistake.

The magic penny, after doubling for thirty days, would in fact be worth a whopping **$5,368,709.12**. The following graph illustrates the value of the penny over time.

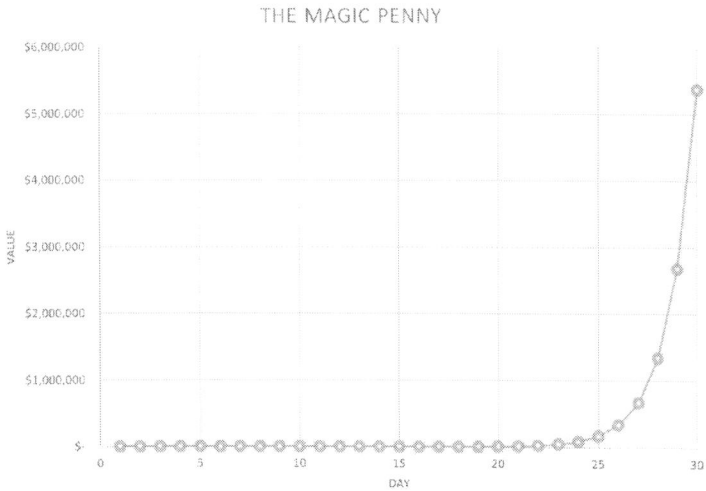

We see that nothing all too noteworthy happens in the first twenty-five days—after which, the value of the doubling penny balloons with each subsequent day. This is the power of compounding at work.

Now, in the real world, money obviously does not double as easily as it does with the magic penny. Nevertheless, the power of compounding applies in a very real way.

In the real world, our magic penny is the stock market.

How quickly can you expect your money to grow in the stock market? Let's consider the S&P 500, a stock market index that measures the stock performance of the 500 largest U.S. companies, which is often used as a proxy for overall market performance. Since its inception in 1957, the S&P has had an average annual return of about 8%. There is some debate around what rate one should use in their long-term projections of market performance. The man himself, Warren Buffett, for example, has said that you should expect, after accounting for inflation and dividends, a 6-7% annual return in the stock market over the long run. Others

2

will use shorter time horizons, such as the past 30 years, during which the S&P exhibited a 10% average annual return. As the general range of returns is somewhere between 6-10%, it seems reasonable to proceed with the long-term S&P annual return of 8%.

Now, how much money would you have today if you invested, say, $1,000 in the S&P in its first year? Assuming an average annual return of 8%, your initial $1,000 investment would be worth **$127,554.73** today.

THE S&P 500

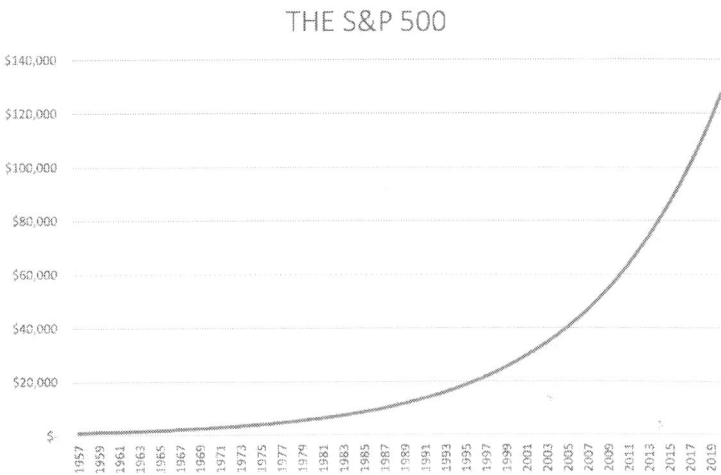

Notice how similar this graph appears to the graph of the magic penny. Both scenarios benefit from the power of compounding, and both scenarios exhibit *exponential growth*. You don't need your money to double every day for it to grow exponentially. The stock market, with its relatively modest 8% return, is sufficient to grow your money exponentially over time.

Before we get into the heart of the matter, let's take a moment to emphasize the fact that 8% is merely a historical average. Volatility is a defining characteristic of the stock market, and in any given year the market will, more likely than not, significantly under or over perform as compared to its historical average. Moreover, past performance does not indicate future results. The future is unpredictable, as we've all been keenly reminded of with the outbreak of COVID-19. Still, given what information we have, the market seems to consistently reward those who invest long-term.

Now, what does all this talk of stocks and investments have to do with passive income? To put it simply:

The stock market is the ultimate passive income machine.

The stock market consistently rewards those who employ a long-term, passive investment strategy such as *index fund investing* (more on this later). More active investors, on the other hand, who use strategies such as *value investing* or *growth investing*, generally face mixed results. Because one of the aims of this book is to serve as a comprehensive analysis of alternative income streams—including those not traditionally considered "passive"—we'll touch on active investing strategies later in this book; however, our main focus will be on the former, as this strategy will enable us to reap the benefits of the stock market with little to no effort.

By simply allocating your money into an ETF (Exchange-Traded Fund) or index fund made to replicate overall market performance, you are able to sit back and watch your money grow. It doesn't get more passive than that.

Say you invest just one dollar every day for thirty years. How much money would you have at the end of thirty years? The answer, assuming an 8% annual return, is **$42,976.56**. At a dollar per day, you will have invested about $11,000 over the course of thirty years, resulting in a profit of about $32,000—just by setting aside one dollar per day! You could put this book down right now, read no further, and you will have already gotten a great deal more than your money's worth.

But the title of this book, after all, is "The Passive Income *Millionaire*," and so we don't get excited by as minor a sum as $32,000.

What if instead of $1 per day, we invest $5? In thirty years, we'd have $214,882.82. If we invest $10 per day, we'd have $429,765.63. So the question becomes: How much would we have to invest per day in order to become a millionaire in thirty years? The answer is about $24 per day. The following chart summarizes the variation in portfolio value given daily investment.

Daily Investment	Total Investment	Value After 30 Years
$1	$ 10,950	$ 42,977
$5	$ 54,750	$ 214,883
$10	$ 109,500	$ 429,766
$20	$ 219,000	$ 859,531
$24	$ 262,800	$ 1,031,438

To reiterate: You would have to invest about $24 per day, or $720 per month, in the stock market for your money to grow to $1,000,000 in thirty years. If you had simply kept that money in a savings account, it would be worth about a quarter of that.

Now, while most of us can spare a couple of bucks every day to invest (which in itself is a good idea), most do not have $720 to invest every month—hence why this book exists. In the subsequent chapters, we will cover the multitude of ways you can develop passive income streams, from royalties to real estate (no, you don't have to own property to make passive income on real estate), and we will learn how to put the money we earn to work by channeling it into the ultimate passive income machine, the stock market.

What differentiates this book from others like it is a continual focus on the most important factor in all of this: the human element.

Let's face it: we are not all the same. Not all of us are cut out for the frugal, ascetic lifestyle preached by other authors; in fact, such a lifestyle, for some of us, would be detrimental to our wellbeing. Saving is certainly a critical factor in long-term wealth. But can't we live a little too? What would be the point in all the hard work we put in to setting up our passive income streams if we have to wait decades to reap any of the benefits?

Many of the books in the market on personal finance read much like ones on dieting, whose bold and promising plans for weight loss are captivating for a short while, but unsustainable in the end. Most of us need a little sustenance, some reward, to motivate us to keep going. And so, in this book, we're going to uncover the sustainable money habits that can set you up to become a millionaire over time, while also allowing you to live a rich and rewarding life along the way.

Let's get straight to it.

We begin by laying the groundwork to our wealth, the *Passive Income Millionaire Framework*.

Section 1: The Passive Income Millionaire Framework

Chapter 1: The Long-Term Investment Horizon Mindset

Let's begin by revisiting the magic penny. In the introduction, we saw how a doubling penny can be worth more than a million dollars due to the power of compounding. What the example of the magic penny also demonstrates is the importance of *investing early*.

Say that instead of the penny doubling for thirty days, it doubled for twenty-nine days instead. Just by missing one day, the value of the penny drops from $5.4M to $2.7M. What if you missed five days? The value drops to roughly $168K.

We can draw parallels to the real word by considering an individual who doesn't invest early. In the introduction, we found that by investing roughly $720 per month, assuming an 8% annual rate of return, our portfolio would grow to over $1,000,000 in thirty years. But what if our time horizon were cut short by five, ten, or even twenty years? What if, alternatively, we were really prudent investors who started at an early age, allowing for a forty-year time horizon? The results are summarized in the following chart.

Time Horizon	Portfolio Value
10Y	$ 131,899
20Y	$ 416,660
30Y	$ 1,031,438
31Y	$ 1,123,057
32Y	$ 1,222,007
33Y	$ 1,328,873
35Y	$ 1,568,935
40Y	$ 2,358,696

Notice that by investing just one year earlier, allowing for a 31Y time horizon instead of thirty, the value of our investment jumps by nearly $100K. Again, we are seeing the power of compounding at work. Alternatively, those who have a slower start do not avail themselves of the benefits of compounding interest, and their returns on investment are more linear than they are exponential. The point has been made abundantly clear:

Invest as early as possible.

And yet, most Americans fail to do so. In fact, 75% of Americans nearing retirement age have less than $30,000 in their retirement accounts. This deeply unsettling figure can at least be partially explained by a phenomenon known in behavioral economics as *hyperbolic discounting*. This fifty-cent term refers simply to the tendency in people to choose smaller, immediate rewards over larger rewards in the future.

Would you rather have $100 today, or $120 one week from now?

Most, falling prey to hyperbolic discounting, choose the former. Our inclination towards immediate gratification is to a certain extent innate, as demonstrated amusingly in the Stanford marshmallow experiment (see YouTube), in which children were offered the choice between a single marshmallow immediately, or two marshmallows after a certain interval. Follow-up studies revealed that those children who were able to wait tended to have higher test scores, lead healthier lives, and have better life outcomes overall.

What distinguishes us from children, of course, is our capacity to overcome our impulses and innate desires through reflection and rational thought. Later in this book, we will go over the various types of investment accounts. If you do nothing else, set up an investment account (if you do not already have one) and allocate a certain portion of your savings to it every month. As we've seen, *small amounts do add up*. Just by investing one dollar per day, you will have already set yourself up for a better retirement than a majority of Americans. And while investing earlier is ideal, it is virtually never too late to reap the benefits of stock-market growth; with a shorter time horizon of ten or even five years, investing in stocks can play a critical part in helping you achieve your financial goals.

Chapter 2: The All-Or-Nothing Pitfall

As humans, we tend to take a pernicious all-or-nothing approach to many of our endeavors. If our dieting and exercise do not result in us looking like swimsuit models or being worthy of the cover of GQ magazine, we give it up. If we decide to pick up a new hobby and do not immediately excel, we lose interest. If we don't get rich quick from whatever scheme the latest prominent guru has cooked up, our interests soon wane.

We are spurred to action by an irresistible image of a better, more perfect self, and we cling to this image at the outset of whatever pursuit we find ourselves in. Time passes, and, to our growing dismay, reality seems stubbornly reluctant to align with our imaged selves. Hope soon fades, and eventually we move on, awaiting the next thing to come along and once again rouse our hopes for a better life . . . and so the cycle goes.

If we can't change our lives all at once, the thinking goes, then there's no point in trying. And so we remain stagnant, unable to improve our situation. The key is to realize that real, positive change can only happen incrementally.

The same applies to our finances. Just because you *can* save more money, doesn't mean you should. If, after an appraisal of your spending habits, you find that you spend too much on, say, eating out or online shopping, and you resolve to cut your spending in these categories by half, you may find yourself rather miserable. The reality that many of us face when it comes to saving is one of *diminishing returns*. If we were to imagine our happiness or, more generally, life satisfaction as a function of how much we save—our *savings rate*—it would probably look something like this:

DIMINISHING RETURNS WHEN SAVING

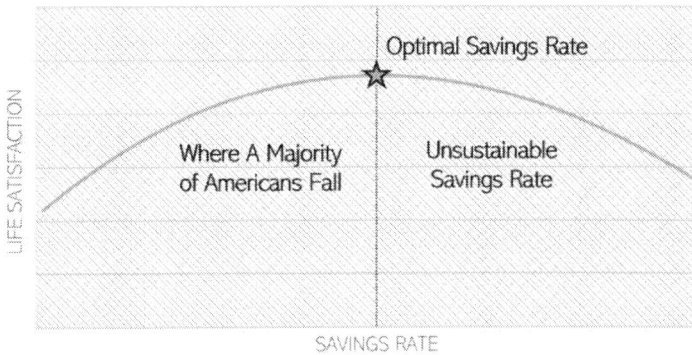

The reality is that most of us are saving less than we should. About 40% of Americans save five percent or less of their annual incomes; one in five don't save *any* portion of their income towards retirement. This is a staggering statistic, considering that it's generally recommended that you save somewhere between ten and twenty percent of your income for retirement. And so it's clear that most of us can benefit by saving more, and by allocating some of these savings towards a retirement or investment account—however, *there is a limit.*

Save too much, and you will begin experiencing diminishing returns on your increased savings; in other words, there is an *optimal savings rate* (as indicated by the star on the previous graph) beyond which you will end up less happy, or more miserable, than you would be if you saved less. Beyond the optimal savings rate we have a range in which you would be saving at an unsustainable rate, likely reverting back to your old, sub-optimal spending and saving habits.

Let's once again draw a parallel to dieting: we have all experienced the strong impulse to quickly get into shape. We react to this impulse by conjuring up a bold plan, one in which we completely change around our eating habits and exercise many more times a week than we would normally. As we find time and time again (and yet seem unable to internalize), because the lifestyle changes we've contrived are such a drastic departure from our normal state, over time we experience a natural correction, or, as folks in the financial world would call it, a *reversion to the mean*. Despite our best intentions, we are eventually overtaken by a ravenous hunger (literally) that seeks to negate all our dieting and progress, until, sometimes, we end up less healthy and less in shape than we were before.

The same applies to our financial health, which is why in this book we are not going to set ourselves up for failure by undergoing drastic changes to our spending/saving habits. This, at last, is where passive income comes in. Passive income is what can enable you to satisfy not only your present self, but also your future self, the one who must ultimately face the realities of retirement. Setting yourself up for a comfortable retirement does not mean you need to make great sacrifices along the way, and passive income can save you from having to make compromises.

Most people believe, as is conveyed in many books and articles on the topic, that their retirement is solely a function of how much of their income they are able to save. The formula implicit in this way of thinking looks like this:

$$R = S_I$$

Put into words: your retirement (R) depends on how much of your income (I) you save over your lifetime. In this book, we are going to be working from a different formula:

$$R = S_I + S_{PI}$$

Here, the amount of money you can expect to have for retirement is a function of how much of your primary income you save (S_I), plus how much you save of income earned through passive income streams (S_{PI}).

Because we are able to save a portion of the money we earn through passive income, this alleviates the pressure that is usually placed on the amount we save of our regular paychecks. In Chapter 5, we are going to introduce the various means of earning passive income, and the remainder of the book will be devoted to examining each type of passive income stream in greater detail.

Before we get there, it is important to remember that individual circumstances vary. In the previous graph, we demonstrated that because of diminishing returns on savings, there is an *optimal savings rate* at which one's life satisfaction is maximized. In realty, everyone's graph is going to look different. Some people are simply cut out to maintain highly frugal lifestyles, and they like it that way. For them, their optimal savings rate is much greater than that of the average person. They are the ones who are able to meticulously monitor their spending, and, in some cases, do not hesitate to resort to what the average person would consider immoderate, such as renting out rooms in their house, or keeping a watchful eye on the temperature to which the thermostat is set (you know who you are!).

For most of us, however, such measures are not worth the inconvenience or sacrifice, and—as we've established—are impractical because they are unsustainable. Thankfully, we are able to bridge the gap through passive income.

Whether you are a penny-pincher or spendthrift, it is critical to understand your existing financial habits, and so in the next chapter we will be taking stock of our finances. With this information at hand, we can begin to understand our individual optimal savings rates, and determine how much passive income we need to earn in order to lead optimal lives.

Chapter 3: Taking Stock of Your Finances

This chapter is divided into two parts. In the first, we will be taking a look at our finances to determine our current savings rate; and in the second, we will be using the data we've compiled in the first section to determine our optimal savings rate.

How much am I saving now? What is my current savings rate?

The topic of the first part of this chapter is typically an uncomfortable one for most, especially those who are not in the habit of budgeting, or who have only a vague idea of their expenses. Have no fear, for you are not alone: according to a recent study by U.S. Bank, only 41% of Americans use a budget. It may serve us well, at this point, to remind ourselves of the popular Chinese proverb:

"The best time to plant a tree was twenty years ago. The second best time is now."

We *know* we should be budgeting; we know we would benefit from simply tracking our financial expenditures from month to month. And yet we still don't do it. The cognitive dissonance that arises from this inconsistency creates in us a kind a financial malaise, which, we must realize, is detrimental to our wellbeing over the long run. By budgeting and having a clearer picture of our finances, we would be better off not only in a fiscal sense, but in a more general, holistic sense—ridding ourselves of the anxiety that builds from the lack of control over our financial situation.

The past is in the past. The benefits that we could have incurred from budgeting, saving, investing (etc.) earlier are a *sunk cost*. All that matters now is that we adjust our behavior today, and continue on the right path moving forward. Fortunately for us, developing healthy financial habits has become easier by leagues thanks to tools that automate most of the heavy lifting. Budgeting apps such as Mint, YNAB, PocketGuard, Clarity Money, and Goodbudget—to name a few—allow you to track your finances with very little overhead; each uniquely appeals to certain types of individuals, so be sure to do some research to identify which is the best for you. (Full disclosure: for the sake of providing you a full and impartial guide, I am not affiliated with any of the tools or platforms mentioned in this book; my intent is in no way to promote any of these products, but to provide the most commonly used and generally well-regarded apps and tools that could potentially assist you in your financial goals.)

Regardless of what tool you use, you will need to perform an initial assessment of your spending and saving tendencies. Let's run through a simple example in which we will determine a hypothetical individual's current savings rate.

Alice is an accountant who earns $4,500 per month in net pay, her take-home money after all deductions. As for her expenses, she begins by categorizing them into the two general categories: fixed and variable expenses. Her *fixed expenses* (rent, car payment, cell phone bill, etc.) are easy enough to determine. Her *variable expenses* (groceries, gas, utilities, etc.) are a bit trickier, and so she pulls up her credit card statements for the past six months and calculates a monthly average for each category, so that in the end all of her expenses over the past half year are accounted for as either a fixed or variable expense; this takes her several hours to do, but she feels accomplished afterwards and rewards herself by ordering sushi.

In the end, her current spending looks something like this:

INCOME	
Net Pay	**$4,500**
EXPENSES	
Fixed Expenses	**$2,050**
Rent	$ 1,200
Auto Loan	$ 250
Car Insurance	$ 60
Student Loan	$ 400
Cell Phone	$ 65
Internet	$ 75
Variable Expenses	**$2,050**
Groceries	$ 400
Fuel/Transportation	$ 300
Utilities	$ 100
Personal care items (drugstore)	$ 150
Eating Out	$ 400
Vacations	$ 150
Clothing/shoes	$ 250
Other	$ 300
Total Monthly Expenses	**$4,100**
SAVINGS	
Total Savings	**$ 400**
Current Savings Rate	**9%**

Half of what she saves every month goes to a savings account and the other half to an investment account. After reading several articles on personal finance, she finds that the general consensus is that one should be saving somewhere between ten and twenty percent for a comfortable retirement, and so she sets as her goal a target savings rate of 15%, or $675 per month. In the beginning she attempts to reach her goal entirely by *saving more*, specifically by eating out less and spending less while on vacation. After a few months, however, she finds these adjustments too cumbersome and ends up reverting back to her old spending habits.

If only Alice had picked up this book! In order to save $675, Alice would need to save about 70% more than she is currently, which is a pretty tall order. Instead, through passive income streams, she could have reduced the burden of saving more by half, say, by saving an additional 3% of her income and earning the remaining 3% through passive income, allowing her to reach her target savings rate of 15%. A savings rate before passive income of 12% is much easier to maintain than one of 15%, and she would have been much more likely to sustain this incremental change in her saving habits.

If you haven't already, run through this exercise on your own, calculating your average spending in these categories over the last six months; the key to keep in mind is that the time period should be representative of your general spending habits. If you haven't taken a vacation in the past six months, for example, determine how many vacations you take per year and how much you spend on each vacation to calculate your yearly vacation spend, and divide that by twelve to determine a monthly average. *All of this will take time.* By doing so, however, you will have taken a major step towards attaining financial freedom, one many are too apprehensive to take. Be sure to reward yourself afterwards for a job well done.

What is my optimal savings rate?

Your *optimal savings rate* is the highest rate at which you can comfortably—and hence sustainably—save money every month. In the previous example, we saw that because Alice's *target savings rate* exceeded her optimal savings rate, she was not able to sustain her target savings goal.

Your target savings rate will likely exceed your optimal savings rate. Attempting to bridge the gap

by forcing yourself to save more is likely unsustainable; instead, supplement your income with passive income to meet your target savings rate.

This is key. Your *target savings rate* and *optimal savings rate* are not the same. Let's consider each in turn.

Your target savings rate is the percentage of your income you should be saving every month. This will vary across individuals, depending on their financial goals. As a rule of thumb, however, one should aim to save around 20% of their income. Many use the **50/30/20 rule**, where 50% of their income goes towards essentials, 30% towards discretionary spending, and 20% towards savings.

Considering that most Americans save much less than 20%, it is easy to see how one's optimal savings rate is lower than their target. If you naturally save about 10% and have done so all your life, you can't expect to suddenly be able to save twice as much. You can probably save at least a little more than you are now, but you will likely still encounter a gap between your optimal and target savings rates.

The key is to start small. Once you've determined your current savings rate, try to adjust your spending habits so that you're saving 1-3% more per month. If you find that you can manage, continue increasing your savings rate until you no longer feel comfortable doing so—at which point, you've found your optimal savings rate. There are some practical steps that you can take along the way to make this easier, which will be outlined in the next chapter. From there, we will learn how to bridge the gap between our optimal and target savings rates by developing passive income streams.

Chapter 4: A Piecemeal Approach to Finding Your Optimal Savings Rate

In keeping with the notion that real, sustainable change only comes about incrementally, we will employ a *piecemeal approach* to increasing the amount we save every month until we've reached our optimal savings rate.

Let's revisit the example of Alice the accountant. After an appraisal of her finances, Alice found that she currently saves on average $400 per month, or 9% of her net income. How much would she have to save to achieve a savings rate of 10%? The difference here is 1% of her net pay, $4,500, which amounts to just $45.

We can clearly see that saving just 1% more of our net pay, in most cases, won't result in a huge difference. Alice finds that she is able to spend $45 less per month by simply cancelling a few subscriptions she no longer really uses. The next month, she decides to increase her savings rate to 11%; however, she is unsure how to cut back.

This is a dilemma that all of us will face as we get nearer to our optimal savings rate. How do you decide exactly how to cut back? How do you decide between spending less on clothes versus dining out? Whether you should take public transportation instead of Ubers? Whether it's worth making coffee at home versus buying from Starbucks?

Needless to say that the answers to such questions vary across individuals. The crucial factor to keep in mind when assessing these questions for yourself is *value*. How much value does a particular good or service bring to you? A common mistake that many individuals make is to identify a category in which they spend a lot of money, such as dining out, and attempt to make drastic cutbacks within that category, never stopping to ask themselves: How much joy or convenience does eating out bring to my life? If I were to eat out half as much, would that significantly impact my life, potentially make me miserable?

The point is, you should *avoid changing around your spending habits too drastically when it comes to the things—whatever they may be—that bring you the most value.* For all those other things that you could do without, cut back as much as possible.

Take a look at everything you've purchased over the past few months and ask yourself: *Did I really need to make this purchase? Would I have been just as well off if I hadn't?*

This exercise, if you're going through it for the first time, will most likely expose the many frivolous things that you waste your money on, and which you could do just as well without. These are the items that you should be ruthlessly cutting from your budget; doing so will then allow you to spend money on the things that make you happy *in good conscience.*

Once you've cut back to the point that you've achieved a leaner budget and would not be comfortable spending much less per month, you've arrived at your optimal savings rate. At this point, there is a critical step that you should take to ensure you continue saving at your optimal savings rate:

Automate your savings.

The best way to save money is to do it mindlessly. Set up monthly automatic deposits from your checking or other deposit account to your savings and investment accounts. Out of sight, out of mind. Automatically saving a certain portion of your net pay will help minimize the *feeling* that you are saving, because it's as if you never had the money in the first place.

It's as simple as that. Now, let's review the steps we took to arrive at this point.

1. Determine your current savings rate
2. Increase your savings rate by 1% of your net pay every 1-2 months until you've found your optimal savings rate
3. Automate your savings so that you are saving at your optimal savings rate every month moving forward (once you begin making passive income, you can adjust the amount so that you are saving at your *target* savings rate)

By looking back at the past six months, we were able to determine how much we tend to save on average. From there, we increased our savings rate by 1% of net pay every 1-2 months, budgeting for the goods and services that bring us the most value and cutting back on everything else, until we found our optimal savings rate. And finally we automated our savings so that we continue saving optimally into the future.

In the next chapter—at last!—we will outline the passive income streams that will enable you to save beyond your optimal savings rate, and spend more on the things that bring joy or convenience to your life.

Chapter 5: Accelerating Your Retirement Through Passive Income Streams

Now that we've laid the groundwork, we are ready to start developing our passive income streams. In the previous chapters, we saw that our *optimal savings rate* is not the same as our *target savings rate*. Generally speaking, our target savings rate should be 10-20% of our net pay from our primary income, and half of what we save should go to a savings account/emergency fund, and the other half to an investment or retirement account (your target savings will depend on your individual circumstances and financial goals, which should be determined with the aid of a financial advisor).

But because our target savings rate is most likely unsustainable—in other words, our optimal, sustainable savings rate is less than our target savings rate—we will now bridge the gap with passive income.

Let's revisit our pal Alice the accountant. By following the steps outlined in the previous chapters, Alice discovered her optimal savings rate to be 12%. She has been saving at this rate for several months now and is confident in her ability to continue doing so well into the future. She has set up automatic transfers so that half of this 12% goes to a savings account every month, and the other half to her 401(k). Furthermore, her employer matches her contributions up to 4%, resulting in a net retirement savings rate of 10% (the six percent she is already allocating to her 401(k) plus the four percent employer match).

Based on her financial goals, Alice has determined that her target savings rate is 20%, meaning she would have to save an additional 8% of her net income per month, or $360 more per month. Through a variety of passive income streams, she goes on to make an extra $600 per month after all deductions. Here is how she decides to allocate her extra cash:

PASSIVE INCOME		
Net Pay	**$**	**600**
Renting out car on Turo	$	100
KDP Earnings	$	250
REIT Dividends	$	100
Student Loan Refinancing	$	50
Other online income	$	100
ALLOCATIONS		
Total	**$**	**600**
Savings Account	$	150
Investment Account	$	300
Discretionary Spending	$	150

As we can see from the chart, Alice has set up multiple passive income streams (all of which we'll review in turn, and more), which furnish her with an extra $600 per month in income. Of this, she saves $450, which puts her actual savings rate beyond her target of 20%, and $300 of her extra income goes to a new investment account which she opens up. Something truly remarkable is happening here that we can't afford to overlook:

By investing a portion of her passive income into the ultimate passive income machine, the stock market, Alice is <u>making passive income on her passive income</u>.

This is how we get the most out of our passive income: by putting it to work so that we are able to generate exponential returns over time.

The passive income—or, more specifically, *investment income*—Alice makes is set up so that it is automatically reinvested back into her portfolio, which of course allows her to take advantage of the *power of compounding interest*. The extra $300, combined with the $450 per month that is already being contributed to her 401(k) every month, results in a cumulative monthly retirement savings of $750—putting her well on track to become a *passive income millionaire*. (Recall that we said you needed to invest about $720 per month at an 8% annual return to achieve a net worth of $1,000,000 over the course of thirty years).

Moreover, Alice has an extra $150 per month to spend on whatever she pleases, which she thinks of as a monthly gift to herself. This month she buys herself the pair of Birdies she's been eyeing for months but whose price she couldn't justify; later she pools together two months' worth of extra spending money to purchase a new bike.

We should be rewarded for the hard work we put in to setting up our passive income streams not only in the future, but today. The amount of extra cash you will have to spend freely will be determined by your allocations and by the number of passive income streams you are able to generate. The hungrier you are, the more you can aim to make in passive income, enabling you to save more aggressively (perhaps for an early retirement), create a certain lifestyle for yourself that you couldn't afford before, or even both.

All of this will be determined by your individual goals. Everyone is different, obviously, which is why a given type of passive income stream is not suitable for everyone. Depending on your interests, proficiencies, willingness to learn, etc., certain passive income streams will appeal to you and others will not. And so for the remainder of this book we will exhaustively cover all of the passive (as well as not so passive) income streams out there. We will leave no stone unturned. The proceeding sections are mutually exclusive, so feel free to jump around as you see fit. We will divide our passive income streams into four categories:

1. Investment Income
2. Online Income
3. Real Estate Income
4. Other Passive Income Streams

Once we've gone through them in detail, we'll review and summarize everything we've learned, and establish immediate next steps. Now, enough prelude. Let's begin with our first main category, *investment income.*

Section 2: Investment Income

Chapter 6: Investment Income That Is Actually Passive

According to a recent study, 89% of fund managers fail to beat the market. This has been the story ever since Burton Malkiel, a Princeton economist, released his groundbreaking book, "A Random Walk Down Wall Street." In it he argues, rather convincingly, that stock prices are random and thus it would be impossible to consistently outperform the market. He even went so far as to say:

"A blindfolded monkey throwing darts at a newspaper's financial pages could select a portfolio that would do just as well as one carefully selected by experts."

This theory has been put to the test many times ever since, perhaps most famously by the Wall Street Journal in their annual Wall Street Journal Dartboard Contest, in which staff members assumed the role of the dart-throwing monkeys. The results, inevitably, put many professionals to shame.

So if a majority of trained professionals with fancy degrees employing state-of-the-art stock prediction techniques fail to beat the market, what chance do you have? The simple honest answer: your odds are pretty slim. Moreover, because a majority of actively managed funds fail to do better than the market, the fees they charge are typically unjustified for a long-term investor, whose investments are better allocated towards low-cost, passively managed funds such as ETFs or index funds.

When it comes to the stock market, it pays to be passive.

Now, let's run through the four major types of investment vehicles:

1. Individual Stocks
2. Mutual Funds
3. Bonds
4. ETFs and Index Funds

When trading individual stocks, also known as *equities*, trade commissions and brokerage fees can really eat into your return on investment. The more often you trade, the more you pay in fees, which is why, in order to minimize fees, one should hold stocks beyond the short term—this, by the way, is a fundamental tenet of Warren Buffet's portfolio strategy.

Mutual funds, as we've already alluded to, are actively managed by fund managers. They allow for greater diversification than picking individual stocks, but incur higher costs, namely management fees.

With *government and corporate bonds*, you are lending money for a certain period of time, being paid interest along the way, typically 2-3% annually, and then receiving the original loan amount when the bond reaches its maturity date. While the interest you are paid is much less than the average return of stocks, bonds are a relatively safe and less volatile investment (you are paid unless the underlying entity defaults, which, in many cases, is unlikely). Given their low volatility, it is generally advised that the closer you are to retirement, the more you should allocate into bonds and away from stocks. The old adage in the investment world is to "own your age" in bonds; for example, if you are 30, 30% of the value of your portfolio should come from bonds, 70% from stocks. If you are 50, 50% from bonds, and so on. As lifespans grow longer and with bond yields potentially lowering, this rule of thumb is proving less relevant, and many now apply the **15/50 stock rule** to their portfolio: if you believe you have at least 15 years to live, your portfolio should be comprised of at least 50% stocks. This strikes a balance between risk and reward, and could potentially allow you to enjoy a longer retirement.

Finally, we have *ETFs* (exchange-traded funds) and *index funds*. The two are very similar and offer similar benefits to investors, and if you are a long-term investor, the differences between the two are essentially negligible. Both offer high diversification, low cost (given they are passively managed), and strong long-term returns. The chief difference between the two is that ETFs can be traded throughout the day, like stocks, while index funds cannot (they are bought and sold only at end-of-day prices); for a long-term investor who isn't trading often, the distinction is moot.

Before we move on, let's quickly touch on **CDs** (Certificate of Deposits). The primary feature of a CD is that it allows you to park your money safely, as it is backed by the FDIC, while offering you more attractive interest rates than a regular savings account. The downside is that you cannot access your funds for a specified period, which can vary from three months to five years (generally, the longer the term, the greater the interest rate). If the only alternative is to store your money in a savings account, and you can afford to not access your funds for a specified period, then CDs can be an attractive option.

Now that we're well acquainted with the types of investment vehicles out there, let's determine which type of investment account is right for us.

Retirement Account vs Normal Brokerage Account

The chief advantage of most retirement plans is the *tax benefits*. With a 401(k), for example, the money you invest is subtracted from your pre-tax earnings, thereby reducing your taxable income and the amount you pay in taxes every paycheck. Furthermore, there is that added benefit of company matching, whereby an employer matches some portion of the employee's contributions. Retirement plans, such as 401(k) plans and IRAs, are essentially made in such a way to encourage you to save for retirement. The downside, however, is that you cannot touch the money you invest until you near retirement age (without incurring a hefty penalty).

Whether you opt for a retirement account or a normal brokerage account—or both—will depend on your financial goals. If your goals are more short or medium term, such as saving for a house or a child's college education, then a normal investment account is the way to go. You are able to access these funds whenever you'd like without incurring huge penalties. If, however, your intent is to invest for retirement, you wouldn't want to forego the tax benefits of a retirement plan.

Retirement Accounts: 401(k) vs IRA

What makes 401(k) plans a no-brainer is the employer match. If your employer offers a company match, be sure to max it out if you can—otherwise you're essentially leaving money on the table. The main downside to a 401(k), as compared to an IRA, is the narrow selection of investment options. With a 401(k), your money is generally invested into various mutual funds, which, as we've seen already, incur higher fees.

IRAs, on the other hand, generally offer a much larger variety of investment options, including index funds and ETFs. The downside with IRAs—there is always some downside—is that you are more limited in the amount you can contribute as compared to a 401(k). To get the most out of the money you are investing for retirement and minimize investment fees, consider opening both a 401(k) and an IRA.

Robo Investing

Let's close this chapter by considering the latest and greatest technological development in the investing world: *robo-advisors*.

Robo-advisors, or automated investing services, use computer algorithms—as opposed to human analysts and money managers—to manage your investment portfolio. By circumventing the need for the personal management of capital, robo-advisors charge much lower fees than human financial advisors: typically between .25% and .5% of your account balance.

Most robo-advisors build portfolios to match the market, meaning they invest your money into ETFs and index funds. Some services claim to employ algorithms that are meant to beat the market, but with mixed results. Whether you are a robo- or human advisor, you will most likely not beat out the market in the long run. And that's totally fine: remember that just by our investments growing at the historical average market return, over time our portfolio will exhibit exponential growth.

When deciding whether to invest your money with a robo-advisor, be sure to compare it with other services that offer varying degrees of financial guidance and, as a result, varying fees. Depending on your knowledge and situation, you may stand to benefit from additional guidance that a financial advisor can provide.

All in all, robo-investing is a strong option for passively maintaining your portfolio. Signing up is fast and simple: typically you fill out a questionnaire to determine your investment goals and risk tolerances, and within minutes you can have an investment account up and running.

Moreover, robo-advisors are able to offer low (sometimes zero) account minimums, as opposed to traditional investment services that sometimes require account minimums in the thousands of dollars. Some robo-advisors to consider include SoFi Automated Investing, Betterment, Wealthfront, Blooom, and Ellevest.

As we move forward into the future, the number and types of automated services will only increase. For example, Acorn is a robo-investment tool that allows for automated investing: rounding up every purchase you make on credit and/or debit cards and investing that money into an account that is managed automatically. You can't get much more passive than that. There is, however, a varying monthly fee you pay to use the app, which, if your account balance is on the smaller side, can constitute an unviable proportion of your total investment. Be on the lookout for new technologies that will inevitably emerge and make investing even more accessible and passive than ever before.

Chapter 7: Not-So-Passive Investment Income

We've established that when it comes to the stock market, it pays to be passive over the long run. A passively managed portfolio of index funds made to mirror market returns will likely pay off in the long run thanks to compounding interest. So the question becomes:

Why bother with active investment strategies when professional investors often fail to beat the market?

While it is highly unlikely for an individual (or even a computer algorithm) to beat the market, it is not impossible. If you consider a large enough set of investors, say 1,000, at least one of them—by virtue of statistical chance—is bound to beat the market over a longer period. Such investors can, retroactively, point to this or that stratagem or insight to justify their success, but we would be hard-pressed to believe that any of them *knew* beforehand that they would beat the market.

Well what about Warren Buffet and Carl Icahn, you ask? What can we learn from their successes in beating the market? The answer, for small-scale individual investors, is very little. These titans of the investment world have access to billions of dollars via their holding companies by which to invest. They don't simply do their homework, wait around to buy stock in a company when it is most undervalued, and leave it at that. The size of their investments is such that they are able to buy managerial authority within the companies, their buy-ins often coming with a seat or two on the board of directors. Their success is as much a testament to their managerial prowess as it is their ability to pick stocks.

Still, for some, there is a certain allure to picking stocks and individually managing at least a certain portion of their portfolio. It can be gratifying to learn the ins-and-outs of various companies. Active investing often affords us a way of staying in tune with the happenings of the greater world around us; we have more to say at cocktail parties or around the proverbial water cooler. Of course, I am certainly not suggesting that being a more interesting conversationalist is a reason to actively manage your investments.

Anyway, for those with this penchant and for the sake of comprehensiveness, let's go over the various equity investing strategies. Equity in stocks need not comprise all of your investment portfolio: we will also review potentially rewarding (though risky) ways to invest your money in privately held companies, such as P2P lending and equity crowdfunding.

Investment Strategy 1: Value Investing (AKA the Warren Buffet approach)

Value Investing assumes that the market is not always efficient, meaning a company's stock price does not always reflect its true worth, or intrinsic value. By buying a stock when it is undervalued, investors seek to gain once the market has corrected itself and the stock price reflects the intrinsic value of the company. Warren Buffet is the paragon of value investing, though this is just one aspect of his overall investment strategy.

There are a multitude of ways to gauge whether a publicly traded company is properly valued by the market, ranging from the basic *price-earnings ratio* (P/E) to more comprehensive analyses. P/E is calculated by dividing a company's stock price by its earnings per share (EPS). A P/E of 1 suggests that the stock is neither over nor undervalued, while a lower P/E suggests that the stock is undervalued, since for every dollar that the company earns, you would be paying less than a dollar for each share you own. We wouldn't want to make investment decisions on P/E ratios alone, however, as accounting methods can often inflate a company's true earnings. A more rigorous analysis of a company's income statements would be necessary to determine the accuracy of its P/E ratio.

There are indexes already out there that specialize in stocks thought to be undervalued, which may save you time if you decide to go with this strategy.

Investment Strategy 2: Momentum Investing (AKA riding the wave)

Momentum investors work under the assumption that winners will continue winning (and losers continue losing). This is among the most active investment strategies, typically reserved for traders who are able and willing to watch stocks on a daily basis, ready to buy or sell at all times. There are, however, funds that one can buy into that employ this strategy. The strategy depends on an ability to *time the market*, which is often a difficult proposition. Moreover, the high trade volume associated with this strategy results in high trading costs, often leading to poor returns net of expenses and fees.

Investment Strategy 3: Growth Investing (What's the next big thing?)

Instead of seeking companies that are undervalued by the market, growth investors want to invest in companies with strong growth potential. Will grocery shopping increasingly be done online in the future? What are the possible applications of virtual reality (VR) technology? Growth investors are constantly looking into the future to assess the growth potential of stocks.

Historically, growth investment strategies have performed worse than value investing over the long run. There are, however, significant periods of time in which growth investing won out—again, we find there is an element of timing required in order to determine those periods that favor growth investing.

Whatever investment strategies you employ, be sure to consider your financial goals and risk tolerances first. Certain strategies are not suited for certain types of investors. Maximize your returns by minimizing trading costs: alternating strategies and switching course too often can be expensive, leading to excessive fees and taxes on any gains.

Investing in Private Companies: P2P Lending and Equity Crowdfunding

Picking and choosing stocks of publicly traded companies is not the only option when it comes to actively managing your portfolio. There are countless private companies and individuals seeking funds for their businesses who are prepared to reward you handsomely for your investment. Lending your money—beyond the relatively risk-free option of bonds—can be a potentially rewarding means of diversifying your portfolio; however, as always, with high reward comes high risk.

Peer-to-peer lending is not a novel concept: people have been lending other people money since the dawn of civilization. With the advent of the internet, however, you are no longer limited to lending to others you know or could potentially seek out locally. Online P2P lending platforms connect you to entrepreneurs and small businesses from around the world; since their emergence in 2005, P2P lending worldwide has swelled to a $34 billion industry according to MarketWatch.

By cutting out the middleman—banks and other financial institutions—investors are able to pocket more of the interest paid by borrowers (though the platforms generally charge a 1% service fee). Furthermore, many of the online platforms assess borrowers' creditworthiness using proprietary algorithms, keeping lenders better informed and better able to manage risk. The platforms generally advise to diversify your investments by lending to multiple borrowers: that way if any one of them goes belly up—which is generally more likely than with larger, publicly traded companies—you will have hedged your portfolio against any losses.

There are many players in the online P2P marketplace, but if you're just getting started, here are some big names to consider: Peerform, Upstart, LendingClub, Prosper, Kiva. Compare the various platforms to determine which works best for you. As with picking individual stocks, you will need to do your homework on individual borrowers—granted you will be working with less information, given these are privately held companies, hence the greater risk. This makes P2P lending a more active, and hence less passive, investment option, though offering returns that are potentially greater than that of the market.

P2P lending is solely concerned with the *debt* side of investing in small businesses, but we must not forget the other form of capital: *equity*. With equity investments, you are buying an ownership stake in the company you are investing in, hoping the value of your equity will grow as the company grows. This is generally much, much riskier than debt investing, though with bigger potential upside.

Equity crowdfunding platforms such as WeFunder, SeedInvest, AngelList, CircleUp, Fundable, and Crowdfunder (to name a few) connect individual investors to small businesses seeking capital. Some crowdfunding websites, like Kickstarter, are not investment platforms, but are "rewards" based, promising you rewards such as a prototype of a new product in exchange for your investment. Such websites will not help you grow your wealth, and should be distinguished from equity crowdfunding platforms.

Investor accreditation and large investment minimums bar many prospective investors from getting involved with equity crowdfunding, but with the passage of the JOBS (Jumpstart Our Business Startups) Act in 2012, non-accredited investors have more investment opportunities than ever before. The policies and limitations vary across platforms, so be sure to understand them when determining which is right for you.

It cannot be overstated that with equity crowdfunding, you are taking on a substantial amount of risk. Most start-ups fail, and thus many early investors lose their entire investment. But if you happen to invest in a "unicorn" such as a Facebook or a Google early on, the payoff could be massive. If you are not prepared to take on such risk, then consider investment options that are generally lower risk such as debt investing or investing in publicly traded companies through stocks.

For individuals with higher risk tolerances and a willingness to put in the time and effort required to perform the due diligence behind selecting individual stocks or start-ups in which to invest, active investing strategies offer greater potential upside than more passive strategies such as index fund investing. The key word here is *potential*, as with greater potential upside comes greater potential downside.

Consider the various means of earning extra income presented in this book along with the alternative investment strategies presented in this chapter. You may find a less risky, more reliable form of income that may not offer the huge potential upside of equity investing, but align more with your risk tolerances.

Section 3: Online Income

Chapter 8: Digital or Physical Products?

With the advent and proliferation of online activity, we have vastly greater opportunities to start businesses or develop alternative income streams than any generation that preceded the internet. Any one of us is just a click away from designers, suppliers, distributors, customers, editors, researchers, experts, etc. from all around the globe, to whom before we would have never had access, and whom we can leverage to advance our online businesses.

Penetrating the world of online business can seem like a daunting task. There are droves of individuals in the marketplace peddling their "unique" methods for earning income online. While it is true that there is a great variety of ways to make money online, we can simplify our approach by breaking them up into two main categories: *digital* and *physical* products.

There are two types of online income: 1) **digital-product income** and 2) **physical-product income**.

No matter what kind of online business you are running, at the end of the day you are selling something. This can either be a hard, physical product or an intangible, digital product. The latter type tends to be more conducive to a passive income approach, and so our focus will be on digital products. We will address this type of online income first: think blogs, podcasts, YouTube channels, eBooks, online courses, etc. These fall under the category of digital products, and we will consider them using a systematic approach that is unique to this book, which we'll refer to as the **Digital Products Business Model**—we'll cover this in greater detail in the next chapter.

In general, what we'll find with digital products is that they require an initial investment of time, effort, and sometimes money. But then, once we automate the process, we're able to enjoy income more or less passively, with occasional maintenance needed to keep our passive income streams flowing and potentially reach more customers.

Within the category of physical products, or e-commerce, we encounter varying degrees of passivity across the various business models: dropshipping, private labeling, retail arbitrage, and so on. One of the chief benefits of certain e-commerce business models is that they are highly *scalable*: you may stand to make a lot more money running an e-commerce store, but when you start to reach that point your online business will start resembling a traditional business, in the sense that it will require very active involvement on your part. Assuming you're more interested in a passive approach, selling physical products online may not be right for you. Still, we'll expand upon the various e-commerce approaches in the last chapter of this section.

Chapter 9: The Digital Store: Mailing Lists, eBooks, Blogs, YouTube, and More

Welcome to your very own *digital store*. Here you essentially sell just one product, and that is **content**. "Content is king"—annoyingly overused, but a pertinent phrase nonetheless. Each product in your digital store takes on a different form of the underlying content, packaged and presented to cater to a specific way in which content is consumed; e.g., blog posts, eBooks, online courses, YouTube videos, podcasts, social media posts, etc.

Like many other stores or businesses, your beginnings are humble. You start out with a **core product**, your bread and butter, the digital product that delivers the greatest value to your audience and which generates you the most revenue. Whether your core product is a YouTube channel, book, or blog is entirely up to you, and it will depend on what you do best. Are you an extrovert who loves to be in front of the camera and have your radiant personality pour through the screen for viewers' pleasure? If so, a YouTube channel may be a right fit, whereby you will earn money through ad revenue and product promotions. Or perhaps you are averse to the limelight, and would rather opt for the thoughtful, systematic approach necessary to write blog posts or books.

Whatever your preferences or propensities, you will need to ask yourself, What do I do best? What do I know, and What would people find interesting? Every one of us has unique knowledge, interests, hobbies, perspectives, or experiences that we can share with the rest of the world. And if you feel stuck or feel you have nothing new to bring to the table, there is nothing stopping you from going out there and acquiring new knowledge or interests that others will find useful. It is not the case that you should only "write [or in certain cases, *record*] what you know." Create from what you know or care to know more about.

Once you've established your core product, *maximizing traffic* becomes the name of the game. You will create **complimentary products**, such as a blog or a YouTube channel, that will drive traffic to your core product, your biggest money maker, and in turn you can reference your complimentary products in your core product, which you will want to do assuming you've *monetized* your complimentary products (through ads, promotions, royalties, etc.). This is key: each product in your digital store should reference and promote the other products, thereby maximizing the revenue that every digital product generates; this captures the essence of the *Digital Products Business Model*.

There are three key features of this model, which are summarized in the following chart.

THE 3 KEY FEATURES OF THE DPBM
A **core product**, such as a book or an online course, that generates the most revenue for you, the digital store owner
One or more **complimentary products**, each of which drives traffic to the core product, and vice versa, and that are ideally monetized
A **mailing list**, or group of subscribers and followers, to which to promote new content

Let's discuss the third key feature in greater detail. If you don't have a mailing list or way of acquiring subscribers, *every sale is a missed opportunity to acquire a long-term customer*. Let that sink in for a moment. Many digital store owners fail to grasp this, rushing to put out their content without realizing its true monetary potential and failing to build up the infrastructure to promote the sale of future content.

According to the Direct Marketing Association, businesses that employ email marketing see a *4300% return on their investment*. For a relatively small monthly fee paid to an email marketing service (Constant Contact, ConvertKit,

Mailchimp, etc.), you'll be able to automatically maintain email lists, landing pages, and send personalized bulk emails through marketing automation. Once you've set everything up, the process is relatively hands-off (or, as we like to say, passive), allowing you to seamlessly convert customers to members of your email audience.

Setting up a mailing list is easy. There are five simple steps that you can follow, outlined as follows:

THE 5 STEPS TO SETTING UP YOUR MAILING LIST

1. Set up an account with an email marketing service
2. Set up a **landing page** where people can opt-in to receive emails
3. Create an **incentive** for people to join your mailing list
4. Reference this incentive in your blog, book, etc. and include a link to your landing page
5. Create a **welcome email** that new audience members will receive once they've opted in, which includes the promised incentive

Setting up a landing page through your email marketing platform is fast and easy, and you don't have to build it from scratch. Browse the web for existing landing pages and base yours off of ones that you like. Once you have a landing page, you'll need to incentive your customers to join your mailing list. Free eBooks, cheat sheets, worksheets, templates, coupons, webinars, and video courses are all common incentives that content producers use to get people to opt in. Of course, you'll need to reference this inventive in your digital product, and include a link to your landing page. Marketing automation allows all of this to happen seamlessly, as people will automatically receive a welcome email along with the inventive once they've signed up.

Once you've followed these steps, your email list will grow on its own with little to no oversight needed on your part. Then, when you are ready to promote your next product, you can send a bulk email to all of your subscribers. Beware, however, of *subscriber fatigue*. You wouldn't want to pester your audience every other day with an email blast, potentially inciting them to unsubscribe from your mailing list. Still, it is important to keep your audience members engaged with content that will actually bring them *value*.

Mailing lists and subscriptions are a core element of the Digital Products Business Model, vital to the sale and promotion of your future digital products. But what are all the types of digital products out there? Which are right for you? And, most important of all, how do you monetize each one to earn a passive income? Let's cover the major digital products one by one, starting with books.

Digital Product #1: eBooks, Audiobooks, and (while we're at it) Paperbacks

Books are the first digital product in this list because writing them aligns most with our desire to develop income streams that are actually passive. Granted, of course, this passive income stream will require an upfront investment of time (the book needs to be written) and, sometimes, money. But once you've written and published your book, there is very little you need to do, except perhaps promote your book, and so you can sit back and watch as book royalties get deposited into your bank account every month.

The #1 platform for publishing your books is undoubtedly Amazon **Kindle Direct Publishing (KDP)**. Roughly two-thirds (this varies across sources) of the US eBook market is comprised of KDP sales. While there are other platforms, especially globally, that you can utilize to expand your reach, KDP is where you want to start.

If you're just starting out and are not sure what to write about or what will sell well, you'll need to perform **market research** to identify a profitable niche. If you're interested in figuring out how to do this, check out my book on the topic, *How to Publish a Book on Amazon: A Bestseller's Guide to Self-Publishing, Formatting, and Marketing Using Amazon Ads*, where I cover everything from market research to promoting your book. Easily access the book by simply visiting my author page on Amazon.

As I've mentioned, getting your book published may require an upfront investment, but this is totally optional. You can pay to have your manuscript professionally edited and formatted and your book cover designed, but there are DIY options out there for those on a tight budget (Canva for cover design, for example). However, a professional touch—especially when it comes to cover designs—tends to make a big difference in your earnings.

Here are the general steps you should follow when publishing your book:

THE 5 STEPS TO PUBLISHING YOUR BOOK WITH KDP

1. Set up a KDP account
2. Perform market research to identify a profitable niche
3. Plan, write, and edit your manuscript
4. Obtain a book cover
5. Upload and publish your eBook and paperback on KDP

While it is not absolutely necessary to set up a mailing list prior to publishing your book, it is highly advised. From the day your book is published, you want to start building your mailing list. It will most likely take a while for your very first digital product to gain traction, but having a mailing list and promoting to your audience will help circumvent the initial period of slow sales for future products.

Let's conclude our discussion on books as a passive income stream by going over some key tips.

6 KEY TIPS FOR PUBLISHING YOUR BOOK WITH KDP

1. *Aim to price your eBook between $2.99 and $9.99.* The reason is that within this range, Amazon pays you a royalty of 70% of each book sale, whereas outside this range it is a mere 35%. The royalty structure is different for paperbacks.
2. *The title of your book will determine its success.* Your book needs to be searchable, and so you should aim to incorporate the most-searched **keywords** related to your book's niche into the title or subtitle.
3. Use **keyword research tools** like Google Keyword Planner (it's free) to determine the most relevant keyword for your book.
4. If you don't already have a mailing list or good way to promote your first book, you can use **Amazon Ads** to advertise your book to Amazon shoppers. This works on a *pay-per-click* basis, meaning you pay Amazon a small fee every time a shopper clicks on your ad, even if they don't buy your book. Make sure your book has at least ten or so five-star reviews before advertising.
5. Incorporate helpful links into your eBook, but not your paperback. This will require two versions of your manuscript, one for eBook and one for paperback. Alternatively, to share links with your paperback customer, you can direct them to your website or blog where you can house any useful links.
6. *Formatting your manuscript* on your own can be a nightmare, and Amazon will suppress your listing for formatting issues. If you are less technically

savvy, it may be worth it to hire a freelancer (from websites such as Fiverr) to handle the interior design of your book.

There is so much more to say on the topic, and it is impossible to condense everything into a handful of tips. This is why I wrote a whole book about publishing on Amazon, so be sure to check it out if this passive income stream appeals to you.

Digital Product #2: Online Courses

The market for online courses is probably much larger and more varied than you think. Instructors are not merely academicians or individuals with highly specialized knowledge; most are just normal individuals with something they're passionate about, who care to instruct others on their area of expertise. There are popular and best-selling online courses out there for meditation, pet care, gaming (chess, poker, Rubik's cube), beauty and makeup, aromatherapy, etc. The point is that with the right equipment and willingness, practically anyone can make a successful online course that appeals to a particular niche.

Again, with online courses, there will be an upfront investment of time and—in this case—most likely money, too. You will need to invest in proper equipment (microphone, camera if you are recording yourself) and software (screen recording, video and sound editing) to create your course, but if you end up creating multiple courses, over time these costs spread out and become negligible.

If you've written a book, the next best step to building your digital store may be to create an online course to accompany the book. This is where we see the vital importance of mailing lists. By buying your book and signing up for your mailing list, customers have already expressed strong interest in the topic, and so naturally many of them are likely to want to further their learning by signing up for your online course.

There are many online course platforms out there, but for beginners I would recommend Udemy. While other platforms charge a monthly subscription fee, Udemy makes its money through each transaction on their site. Their cut of the sales made through searches and promotions on their site is 50%, which is quite steep, but for any traffic that you direct to the site (e.g., a reader of your eBook clicking on a link that you provided to your online course) your share of the earnings is **97%**. If most of your sales are direct sales made as a result of your own promotions, this can be an attractive option.

Courses run anywhere between $19.99 (though it can be made cheaper with discounts; i.e., coupons) and $199.99. Generally, your earnings per sale with online courses is much higher than with book sales, and so you don't have to make as many online course sales to match your book earnings. Once you've set up your course, you can earn income passively with little to no oversight, though it would probably be in your best interest to regularly promote your course by advertising or by using coupons.

We'll end our discussion on online courses with some key tips.

5 KEY TIPS TO CREATING AN ONLINE COURSE

1. *Perform market research to ensure there is high demand for you course topic.* On Udemy, you can see for any course the number of students it has had over its lifetime and when the course was created. You can use these two data points to estimate course sales per month.
2. *You are allowed several bullet points in the "What you'll learn" section of the course description—use them all.* The more you have here, the greater the

perceived value customers will feel when deciding to buy your course.

3. *Include downloadable resources—cheat sheets, worksheets, spreadsheets, etc.— and quizzes to keep your students engaged.* With downloadable resources and quizzes, you have an opportunity diversify your course and deliver greater value to your students.

4. *Brace yourself for the editing process.* Sometimes, editing your online course can take just as long as filming/recording. Removing background noise, editing out mistakes, adding titles and images, etc. can all take a while if done well. Be sure to use good video and sound editing software to make your life easier.

5. *Use coupons to promote your course.* The price point of online courses can be too steep for many potential customers; use coupons to discount your course and obtain students that you wouldn't have been able to otherwise.

Digital Product #3: Blogs

Blogging is lower on this list because maintaining a blog, for obvious reasons, is not something you can do passively. Moreover, monetizing the blog itself is not easy to do and can often take years of building up an audience before you see attractive returns on your time. Nonetheless, blogs play a vital role in the digital stores of many online entrepreneurs, serving as a complimentary product that directs traffic towards their more profitable products, such as books or online courses.

There are multiple ways in which you can monetize a blog— affiliate marketing, ads, sponsorships, and memberships being the most common. Let's review each of these in turn.

Chances are, you've heard of **affiliate marketing** before, the process by which you recommend a product to your audience on your blog and receive a commission whenever someone uses a link from your site to buy the product. This can be a fickle means of income, as many online shoppers do their research on multiple sites before deciding to buy a product. With affiliate marketing, you often do the work of convincing a customer to buy a product, but receive no compensation for it as they happen to not use your referral link when they ultimately make the purchase. Still, affiliate marketing makes up a vital component of blog monetization; a survey conducted by VigLink showed that a majority of online merchants were making 5-20% of their revenue through affiliate marketing.

Commission can range anywhere from 15% to 70%. Consider the types of products your readers may be interested in and that align with your blog and brand. Obviously, if you are attempting to sell something like hunting equipment to readers of a personal finance blog, they may find it intrusive or annoying and put off from reading your blog ever again. Once you've determined a product that would make sense for an affiliate marketing campaign, determine if the company has an affiliate program that you can sign up for.

For most blogs, **advertising** brings in the most dough, the two major streams of ad revenue coming from Google AdSense and selling banner ad space directly to advertisers.

Google AdSense is the greatest revenue generator for many blogs. It is easy to set up and in itself a way of generating revenue passively, paying you (a small amount) every time an ad is clicked on your site. However, you can potentially stand to make more by cutting out the middleman and selling ad space directly to advertisers, though this will require a more active effort as you must negotiate price and terms of agreement on your own.

If you prefer your blog or website to be ad-free, you can still monetize through sponsorships or memberships. With

sponsorships, you are still promoting products to your readers, but you also have control over what products you are promoting, unlike with ads, allowing much of the same control over what companies or products your blog is associated with as affiliate marketing. A company pays you to use and talk about their product, and you don't have to rely on readers clicking a link to get paid.

Finally, you can monetize your blog by charging **membership** fees for readers to access premium content. This approach, though less common, may be highly profitable in certain niches. It is probably the least passive way of monetizing your blog, as it will require you to continuously produce premium content to justify the subscription costs that your most loyal readers are paying.

While there are several ways to monetize your blog, doing so should probably not be your first priority. It is more important to first build your audience and minimize the chances of people getting put off from your site by excessive ads and promotions. Once you've built your audience and have consistent traffic to your site, it will be easier to determine how to best monetize your blog.

Digital Product #4: YouTube Channel

Once you've collected 1,000 subscribers to your YouTube Channel and have exceeded over 4,000 watch hours over the past year, you can begin collecting ad revenue by joining the YouTube Partners Program. The amount you get paid isn't determined directly from view or subscriber counts, but from whether viewers click on ads or watch them in full (except if the viewer is watching with a YouTube Premium account, in which case you get paid by the view).

However, the top earners on YouTube are making most of their money not through ad revenue, but through sponsorships and merchandise sales. Here we start straying away from "passive" income, as maintaining a profitable

YouTube channel in itself is often a full-time job. Obtaining 1,000 subscribers is no easy feat, and will require a regular output of high-quality content for some time. Still, your YouTube channel—even if not itself monetized—can play a big role in driving traffic to the high-revenue-generating products in your digital store.

Nearly 5 billion videos on YouTube are watched every day, with over 30 million visitors per day.

This blows the number of blog readers and podcast listeners out of the water. Just by uploading a few videos and getting modest view counts in the hundreds or thousands, you will be able to generate a tremendous amount of traffic to the other products in your digital store. With this sort of business model, it's clear to see that ad revenue on YouTube is negligible and obtaining the requisite 1,000 subscribers is likely not worth the effort. Still, if you enjoy making YouTube videos or are driven to make alternative income in a more active manner, by all means YouTube away!

To say one last thing on the topic, YouTube channels tend to work well with online courses. If you've already spent the time and effort to create an online course, a quick and easy way to promote your course would be to upload snippets of it as YouTube videos. With a comprehensive online course, you are likely addressing multiple pain points or topics of interest for your audience; determine the ones of greatest interest or the ones that are searched for the most and create a YouTube video addressing the specific topic. For example, for a comprehensive course on passive income, we could post a short and useful video detailing the steps to publishing an eBook. This is a hot topic right now, and we are sure to expose our course to a wide audience. Obviously, the video itself needs to be *useful* to viewers and needs to solve a specific pain point—this is your opportunity to demonstrate to potential customers of your digital store the quality of your content, and that they would benefit from buying your book or online course. Upload the very best content from your course, and you are sure to drive ample traffic to your products.

Digital Product #5: Podcasts

Finally, we arrive at the last product in our digital store: podcasts. While certainly not rivaling the massive audience base of YouTube, the podcasting industry has experienced tremendous growth over the past few years, with nearly 70 million weekly podcast listeners as of 2020. The popularity of podcasts is likely to continue grow, making this digital product and its unique audience base worth considering.

As with other products in our digital store, podcasts can be monetized in similar ways: ads, sponsorships, memberships, etc., the specifics varying across platforms. You'll want your podcast to be on all the major platforms (iTunes, Spotify, Google Podcasts, Stitcher, etc.), and you can convert your podcasts (or quality snippets from your podcast) to YouTube videos, a quick and easy way to further expand your online presence.

As with YouTubing and blogging, maintaining a podcast will require an active effort, and may not be in line with your goals, especially if you are looking to develop more passive streams of income. Continuously recording new content, finding potential guests, conducting interviews, editing episodes, etc.—maintaining a quality podcast is a tall order, and many have made a full-time job of it. As with YouTube, there is a certain allure about it that you won't find with the more distanced exercise of blogging or writing in general. Having your voice broadcast for the listening pleasure of hundreds or thousands may appeal to you, in which case you may want to consider podcasting as a means of building your digital store.

In this chapter, we've covered the basics of growing and running your very own digital store in accordance with the *Digital Products Business Model*. There are countless variations of this online business model, which are determined by how you configure your digital products in relation to each other to drive revenue. But at a high level, you generally have one (or potentially more) *core products* that deliver the greatest value to your audience and that bring you the most revenue. The remaining *complementary products* serve to drive traffic to your core products, but can be themselves monetized as well (generally through ads, affiliate marketing, and sponsorships). Together all of the products in your digital store exist in a symbiotic environment, promoting each other and expanding your reach across the various types of content platforms.

As we've seen, the degree of passivity or active involvement required to maintain a digital store varies. Obviously, one expects to be compensated in proportion to the effort they put in, and it is possible to make a living from your digital store. But for those interested in a more passive approach, there are innumerable niches and opportunities out there to set up income streams that require little to no oversight after an initial input of time and effort.

Chapter 10: Is Running an E-Commerce Business Truly Passive? The Realities of Wholesaling, Dropshipping, and Amazon FBA

As we've seen with the *Digital Products Business Model*, it is certainly possible to establish passive income streams online. But what about *physical products*? What's the deal with all the various e-commerce models out there, like dropshipping, private labeling, print-on-demand, etc.?

In general, running an e-commerce store does not lend itself to *passive* income.

Considering the many tasks required to run a typical e-commerce business—product research, finding and negotiating with suppliers, shipping, marketing, inventory management—we can quickly see that doing so will require a much more active effort. While we are chiefly concerned in this book with passive income, since we are on the topic of online income and since many of you have probably wondered about e-commerce, we will explore the major e-commerce models, with a particular emphasis on level of effort, risk, and potential payoff.

The major e-commerce models, in rough order of increasing complexity, are as follows:

1. Wholesaling
2. Dropshipping
3. Print-on-demand
4. Private labeling (and Amazon FBA)

All four models can be implemented using your own online store; with private labeling, you are not required to have an online store and can sell exclusively on Amazon. Let's take a closer look at each e-commerce model.

E-commerce Model #1: Wholesaling

With *wholesaling* (as well as with dropshipping and print-on-demand) you will be reliant on your online store for income, and so you can think of it as building your business from the ground up (with private labeling, as we'll see later, you can hit the ground running faster by leveraging Amazon's existing massive customer base). This will require a lot of up-front work in building up your customer base and driving traffic to your online store.

With wholesale, you are simply buying product inventory from existing brands at wholesale prices, and then turning a profit by selling individual units at retail prices on your online store. Profit margins with wholesaling tends to be higher than with dropshipping, the major downside being that your money is tied up in inventory. The minimum order quantity set by manufacturers varies, and if you have limited cash to begin your business, you may be limited to selling only a few products in the beginning.

E-commerce Model #2: Dropshipping

With dropshipping, you are selling products that you don't actually own. None of your money is tied up in inventory, and every time a customer puts in an order on your online store, you in turn put in an order with the manufacturer or dropshipping partner, who fulfills the order. The advantages of dropshipping over wholesale is that start-up costs are lower, you can more easily add products and diversify your online store, and the dropshipping partners handle the fulfillment process, including shipping. The cost of all this convenience, however, is slim profit margins. You'll have to sell a significant amount of volume before seeing attractive profits.

Dropshipping is often an attractive option for those just getting started and with little funds to invest in their business. Given the low barriers to entry, however, you will find yourself competing with countless other dropshippers all around the world. It is vital to identify a specific and profitable niche, and to build a brand and sell relevant products that cater to that niche.

Dropshipping and wholesale are not mutually exclusive.

Each product in your online store can be managed differently. A risk-minimizing approach that you may want to consider is to experiment with dropshipping at first, and then if a product proves to sell well, increase your margins on that product by transitioning from dropshipping to owning your own stock.

E-commerce Model #3: Print-on-demand

For those with a creative orientation and interested in graphic design, *print-on-demand* is a type of dropshipping model in which you sell custom designs on various products, such as t-shirts, mugs, phone cases, pillows, and so on. If you don't have any graphic design skills, you are not totally barred from entering this space; there are countless freelancers on websites like Fiverr with whom you can work to create your designs.

Because print-on-demand is a specific type of dropshipping model, none of your money is tied up in inventory and orders are placed with your print-on-demand partner as your customers place them. If you're interested in starting a print-on-demand store, consider the various third-party printing suppliers out there to get started (Printify, SPOD, Printful, and T-Pop, to name a few).

E-commerce Model #4: Private Labeling

Private labeling is similar to wholesaling in that it commits you to own stock in your product. What distinguishes the two is that with private labeling, you are developing your own product and your own brand, soliciting manufacturers to produce your product(s) according to your specifications. Clearly, this is a more involved business model, as you are in charge of the design and marketing of your product. What has catapulted private labeling as a major online business model is the increasing popularity of *Amazon FBA* (Fulfillment by Amazon), whereby you ship your privately labelled products to Amazon's warehouses and sell on their website by maintaining your own product listings.

With private labeling, FBA certainly isn't the only option. With e-commerce platforms like *Shopify*, the idea is that you build your online store from scratch. While you may experience higher margins running your own online store—considering Amazon takes a substantial cut of your profits—the big challenge will be to drive sufficient traffic to your website. Marketing is completely on you, and it can be very difficult to build a customer base from nothing. Many private labelers sell through Amazon FBA and run their own online store, raising brand awareness through Amazon and then eventually making stronger sales on their online store.

If you're interested in learning more about private labeling and Amazon FBA, you can check out my book covering everything you need to know about selling on Amazon (simply visit my author page on Amazon). While this is certainly not a means of making passive income—especially in the beginning, as you are setting everything up and determining your first products to sell—it can be an attractive option for those interested in running an e-commerce business.

This concludes our discussion on online income. Whether you are interested in passively maintaining a digital store, or are looking to build an e-commerce business, there are countless opportunities for you to develop income streams online. Each of the various means of earning income is a massive topic in itself, and a single book can only survey the various business models and approaches. There are countless resources available online and whole books devoted to each specific topic, so be sure to check them out once you've determined the kind of online business you'd like to pursue—which I hope this book, at least, has helped you to do.

Section 4: Real Estate Income

Chapter 11: Rental Income, The Basics

Real estate prices tend to rise steadily over time, which is why buying property has traditionally been thought of as a good investment. The US housing market combines relatively low volatility with returns that are comparable with that of the stock market. Recessions and other crises, however, have recently challenged the age-old assumptions behind real estate investing. Prices don't always rise over time, and sometimes they can drop, taking the value of your investment down with it.

But it's important to look beyond national trends and averages and consider the realities in the specific area in which you are looking to invest. Downturns in the market tend to hit certain areas harder than others, and rebounds in more bustling, metropolitan areas can mask slow recoveries in other parts of the country. The economic realities of the area in which you are looking to buy may not be reflective of the broader market. Be sure to speak with a real estate agent to get a better understanding of the local market.

In general, there are three types of real estate investing: owning, renting, and flipping. *Home ownership* is typically a long-term investment; owners are shielded from any short-term price volatility, and usually turn a profit once they sell the home as a result of steady, long-term appreciation. It is generally advised to have paid off your own home *before* investing in other real estate (defaulting on your mortgage should obviously be avoided at all costs, and you wouldn't want fluctuations in your real estate business to affect your ability to make payments).

Flipping a house can be attractive to some investors given the quicker turn-around time. Generally, flippers buy a home on the cheap, make improvements, and then sell it with the expectation of turning a profit after any and all expenses incurred to renovate the home. This can be a pretty risky venture, and if the market isn't right, you can stand to actually lose money. Moreover, flipping a house is a highly *active* endeavor—think of all the updates and renovations, hiring contractors, making certain updates yourself—and thus will not be highlighted in this book.

Renting property, on the other hand, is more passive in nature. In fact, rental income is the first thing most people think of when considering ways to make passive income. The basic idea is that you buy a turnkey property (or one that needs only minor repairs) at a bargain price, rent it out to tenants while fulfilling your responsibilities as a landlord (e.g., maintenance repairs), and earning income through rent and appreciation of property value.

Many prospective investors are so transfixed by the income potential of maintaining a rental portfolio that they overlook the realities of being a landlord. There are many factors to consider when determining whether rentals are a good passive income choice for you, and in this chapter we'll consider the most important ones. If by the end of this chapter you believe rental income may be a good fit, I encourage you to proceed to the following chapter, where we'll review advanced strategies that can help you hit the ground running.

The Challenges of Landlordship

In reality, as a landlord you will experience fluctuations in the level of involvement and time spent out of your day in maintaining your rental properties. In other words, there are periods in which you can sit back and collect rent, enjoying healthy positive cash flow, and periods in which everything seems to go wrong all at once: broken heater, unpaid rent, a vacant property, etc. Being a landlord can be a stressful vocation, and requires a certain mental fortitude if you are to be successful.

As you scale your rental business or begin to maintain properties outside your local area, many of the day-to-day pains of maintaining rentals can be handled by a *property management company*, but the fees that they charge are typically not feasible for those just starting out with one or two properties. Many landlords just starting out do most of the maintenance and repairs on rental properties themselves.

In the best-case scenario of having perfect tenants, who always pay their rent on time and are respectful of the property, you may still find yourself responding to calls at odd hours in the night. When a pipe bursts or a heater is busted, you are the one responsible for ensuring any repairs or replacements are made in a timely manner. Furthermore, bad tenants can really make your life miserable, missing rent, damaging property, calling you incessantly and unnecessarily, and even forcing you down the cumbersome path of eviction. When finding tenants, it is well worth the investment to *thoroughly vet prospective tenants*, running credit and background checks, thus maximizing your odds of having responsible tenants.

Finally, you may find yourself in a situation where you struggle to fill a vacant property. The rental market in your area may have been strong at one point, but circumstances change, and some factor outside of your control—for example, lower interest rates turning people away from renting and towards buying—may influence your ability to find tenants. Ensure you are prepared for this financially and other surprises (such as major repairs) by setting aside a fifth or even a third of your rental income to weather the storms.

Buying Rental Properties: Cash or Financing?

Speaking of finances, does it make more sense to buy an investment property outright or finance it with a mortgage? This depends on your financial situation, the amount of capital you have to invest, and your financial goals. There are pros and cons to both options, but in general, the main difference is that with buying, you generally incur higher positive cash flow, whereas with financing you receive a greater return on your investment.

When you buy outright, you avoid having to pay any interest (on a mortgage) and thus pocket more of the money coming in through rent. Let's say you buy a home for $100,000, which you rent out, earning $1,000 per month after all expenses. At the end of the year, you will have earned $12,000, or a 12% annual return on your original investment. Instead, if you were to finance the same home, putting down a 20% down payment, you can expect to make a lower monthly income after your mortgage payment, say $300; you will have earned an annual net income of $3,600 on a $20,000 investment, or 18% annual return—lower monthly income (or cash flow), but higher annual return.

Now, you may be thinking, Why care about percentages? Wouldn't I always just want to maximize the *amount* of income I am making? Consider that in the previous example, you only had to invest $20,000 in the second scenario as opposed to $100,000 in the first scenario. Many new investors do not have the funds to buy a property outright, and financing makes real estate investing accessible to those who otherwise couldn't penetrate the market.

But say you did have $100,000 to invest. By buying a property in cash, all of your money will be tied up in that single property, whereas you could potentially make your money go further through financing (also known as *leveraging*). Say, instead of buying one property in cash, you finance several properties. Continuing the above example, instead of buying a single property for $100,000, you could make a $20,000 down payment on five properties. At $300 per month per property, you would net $1,500 per month instead of $1,000 on the one home you bought in cash. Furthermore, now you have five properties *appreciating in value* instead of just one, which could potentially result in huge returns if/when you sell the homes.

The above example is meant simply to illustrate the potential of leveraging. While it may seem like an attractive option to finance five homes on paper, in reality this is a massive undertaking and will require an experienced hand to execute. Obviously you would want to start small: if you prefer not to tie up all of your money in one property (or simply cannot afford to do so) and would like to take advantage of leveraging, you can start by financing just one property, then with experience scale your business and grow your rental portfolio by financing further ones.

Finding The Right Property

There is a lot of general advice out there for finding the right rental property, but this advice can often be vague and even contradictory. For example, "buy local" and "buy low cost" is not possible if you live in an expensive real estate market. In such markets, a rental business may not even be feasible if mortgage payments exceed rent. Still, there is a good amount of sense behind the advice to buy local. As a first-time buyer looking to maintain the rental property yourself, it would only be feasible to buy local. Maintaining properties long distance can be a hassle in itself, requiring a property manager or a trusted team of contractors, repairmen, etc. Still, if your local real estate market is too expensive and you are not able to buy anything in cash, looking elsewhere may be your only realistic option.

Buying a low-cost home is important in order to maintain operating costs and achieve an attractive margin (especially if you are financing), but you should also avoid *fixer-uppers*. Repairs and renovations will likely cost you more than it would experienced landlords, as they have already established a network of trusted and fairly-priced contractors. Consider instead a home that is priced below market value and requires only minor repairs.

The ideal real estate market is one that is up-and-coming, growing but not high cost, with low property taxes, good schools, a growing job market, public transportation, etc. As with markets in general, a real estate market that is too saturated will not offer attractive appreciation potential, and may be difficult or unfeasible to penetrate given already high property values.

Now that we understand the basics of rental income, let's proceed to "the advanced stuff" and expose ourselves to some of the complexity and nuance in running a rental business.

Chapter 12: Rental Income, The Advanced Stuff

In this chapter, we'll run through ten keys tips to bear in mind as you begin your rental business. Many landlords just starting out often overlook the following items, and pay the price later on by learning their lesson the hard way. Follow these ten tips and you will be in better position to excel in your rental business.

Advanced Tip #1: A quality rental listing will attract quality tenants

With this first one, we are essentially talking about *marketing* your rental property. The better your listing, the sooner it will go off the market and the better the tenants that will be attracted to your property. Many first-time landlords rush through this step to get their property out on the market as fast as possible, but this can often have the reverse effect whereby a poor listing fails to attract enough traffic and stays on the market longer.

As with any type of online listing, whether it's a rental or an Amazon product, *photos* are the most important aspect your product listing. Prospective tenants usually scan through the images first, deciding pretty quickly from the images alone whether or not they like the property (first impressions are everything, after all). Therefore it is critical that your listing contains high-quality images that showcase the best features of your rental property.

A professional photographer or expensive equipment are not necessary; nowadays many smartphone cameras are sufficient for taking high-quality photos. Ideally you would want the place furnished (if there are existing tenants in the property, be sure to give them 24 hours' notice). Stage the property as best as you can, opening up the curtains (of course, you would want to take photos during the daytime and with all the lights on), cleaning up any clutter or messes, arranging pillows and other household items neatly. Photograph every room and stand at the widest vantage point to include as much of the space as possible. Take photos of the exterior as well, the most important photo being that of the facade: photographs taken during sunset with all the lights on in the house tend to look the best. Finally, be sure to edit your photos, adjusting the brightness or cropping if necessary to ensure the highest-quality images.

Beyond photos, ensure that the descriptions in your listing are informative, highlight the best features of your property, and are clear and free of grammatical or spelling errors. Research high-quality listings in your idea to get a feel for how it's done and use them as a template for your own.

Your rental listing is the first interaction that prospective tenants will have with you and your rental business. Start off on the right foot with a quality listing, and your odds of landing quality tenants—who will make your job as a landlord much easier—will almost certainly improve.

Advanced Tip #2: Get landlord insurance

You may think that your existing *homeowner's insurance* will cover any major damage to your rental properties. Well, it doesn't. Homeowner's insurance only covers a property that is occupied by its owner; to get the same type of coverage for your rental properties, you need **landlord insurance**.

At the very least, your landlord insurance should cover *property damage* (in the event of a natural disaster, sever storm, fire, damage by tenants, etc.), *liability protection* (in case a tenant is injured as a result of an issue with the property), and *lost rental income* (which covers lost rental income in the event that your property becomes temporarily uninhabitable). Depending on the type of property and the area you are in, you may benefit from certain types of extra coverage, such as flood insurance, emergency coverage (like a pipe bursting), guaranteed income insurance (which may come in handy if you tend to have tenants who are unable to pay rent in full or at all), and more. These are add-ons that may save you money down the road if—or *when*, rather—there are surprises.

Landlord insurance is generally more expensive than homeowner's insurance because rental properties are considered to be more liable to damage than owner-occupied properties. Determine whether any of your existing insurance providers offer *bundling discounts*, as this could potentially reduce your premium.

Advanced Tip #3: Require renters' insurance

Landlords and property managers alike typically require tenants to obtain *renters' insurance*, which covers tenants' belongings in the event of damage. It is generally in the best interest of both the landlord and the tenants for the latter to have renters' insurance. It's low cost, will benefit the tenants if their belongings are damaged, and will prevent situations in which tenants seek litigation and come after you if their belongings are damaged.

Advanced Tip #4: As a landlord, taxes are your friend

One aspect of a rental business that makes it financially attractive is the tax benefits. Rental income is taxed as ordinary income, but there are several ways in which you can reduce your tax burden.

First off, rental income is not subject to self-employment tax; in other words, you don't pay social security of Medicare taxes on your rental income. Furthermore, there is a long list of expenses that you can deduct, including mortgage interest, insurance costs (landlord insurance), HOA fees, property taxes, maintenance costs, depreciation, and more. Most of these are pretty straightforward and go a long way in reducing your tax burden, but let's take a moment to discuss *depreciation* in greater detail.

Depreciation is one of the best tax advantages available to landlords.

Residential rental properties are deductible over a 27.5-year period (commercial rental properties over 39 years). So if you purchase a residential property for, say, $100,000, you can divide this (minus land value, as only the property itself is allowed to depreciate) by 27.5 to get your annual depreciation deduction. If the land is worth $10,000, this comes out to a deduction of roughly **$3,270**. Say your net rental income before depreciation is $5,000; after depreciation, your rental income for tax purposes becomes $1,730—even though your actual profit (or cash flow) is significantly higher. In this way, many profitable rental businesses get away with paying very little in taxes, on paper (thanks to depreciation) appearing to not be very profitable.

Be sure to maximize your deductions during tax time, and don't forget to consider *depreciation* in your calculations.

Advanced Tip #5: Stay organized and maintain digital records

Speaking of taxes, tax time is much less of a headache if you have maintained an organized record of all your income and expenses. The more effort you put in to stay organized, the more time and headache you will save yourself, not only during tax season, but in the event that legal issues arise with your tenants or if you get audited. Furthermore, you may get away with simply organizing your paperwork if you have one or two properties, but once you start managing more it becomes all the more beneficial to maintain digital copies of everything. This allows you to quickly organize your records—such as security deposits, rent payments, maintenance receipts, applications, etc.—into digital folders and search them later on (as opposed to sifting through mountains of paperwork).

Advanced Tip #6: Perform due diligence on a neighborhood before buying

There are many features of a neighborhood that you should assess before buying, some quantitative and others not. *Average rent, vacancy rate,* and *property taxes* are examples of quantitative attributes that you would want to estimate when researching the market. Usually you can find average rent and rental vacancy rates for a given municipality online.

You will need to know the *average rent* of a neighborhood or municipality to determine whether renting is even feasible, and whether rent will cover your mortgage expense, maintenance, etc. You can then use average rent to gauge the rent that you would charge for a specific property and estimate your margins. Bear in mind that average rent is not a static variable: it changes over time, and so you need to understand where the market is headed to ensure rent prices will remain attractive for rental property investors. If average rent prices are increasing, or there is an expected increase as a result of, say, a major company moving to the area, then the area may be worth investing in.

The *rental vacancy rate* is also an important metric to understand, and will help you gauge whether to expect longer periods of vacancy. Obviously, the lower the vacancy rate for an area, the better. Compare the vacancy rate to the broader geographical area (the U.S. Census Bureau compiles a quarterly report on vacancy data), and, as with average rent, understand how the vacancy rate is changing over time to ensure you are making a good long-term investment.

Property tax is another quantitative variable that is easy to obtain. Higher property taxes will obviously eat into your margin, but a high property tax may indicate an attractive area for rental property investors, with higher average rent and lower vacancy rate, allowing you to charge more for rent and potentially deal with better tenants.

Beyond the quantitative factors, there are a number of qualitative factors that you should expect to uncover during market research, such as quality of local schools, crime, local amenities, the job market, and so on. Perform your due diligence and develop a solid understanding of each of these in order to form a complete picture of a local real estate market.

Advanced Tip #7: Know the law

It is important to have at least a basic understanding of *landlord-tenant laws* in your state and municipality, which vary from area to area. To avoid potential legal issues or areas of ambiguity, read up on your obligations as a landlord, such as those having to do with security deposits, disclosure of owner information, maintenance and upkeep, and eviction rules. Know the law ahead of time and avoid having to learn about it the hard way.

Advanced Tip #8: Set up online rent pay

Rental payments—and bill payments in general—are increasingly done online. Online rent pay is convenient not only for landlords, but for tenants as well, who benefit from paying conveniently and safely online (as opposed to mailing checks, which is always a risky practice). Moreover, there is the added convenience of automated payments. The easier and more convenient you make it for your tenants to pay rent, the likelier they will be to pay on time.

Advanced Tip #9: Don't forget to renew your leases

You should be proactive about renewing rental agreements, especially if you have good tenants that you would like to keep. Enquire about 90 days in advance of the end of the lease whether they would like to renew; this will help you avoid vacancies and keep good tenants. Moreover, renewing a lease will give you an opportunity to *raise rent*. Houses appreciate over time, and rent prices follow suit. Be sure to watch average rent prices in your area and the value of your property over time—and increase rent accordingly.

Advanced Tip #10: Establish pet deposits and pet rent

Many landlords are apprehensive about pets and the hassle they can create—property damage, noise complaints, allergens—and thus disallow pets entirely. Roughly half of landlords don't allow for any pets, which is a shame considering about 70% of U.S households have a pet. Clearly there is a gap between demand and supply, which means that landlords who do allow pets can charge more, namely through *pet deposits* and *pet rent*.

Not all pets are the same, and some are a greater liability than others. Consider allowing for certain types of pets (based on the animal, breed, size, etc.) to minimize any risk of property damage while benefiting from charging more in rent.

And there it is. By now, you should have a fairly good understanding of whether rental property investing is right for you, and of the realities of landlordship. Given the rate of appreciation that real estate has historically exhibited, combined with relatively low volatility, real estate competes with equities as an attractive, long-term investment. Of course, the major downsides are that real estate property is a relatively illiquid asset and requires a considerable upfront investment, tying up your cash and precluding other investment options. But if you have it takes to become a landlord and the cash to invest, real estate investing may be a solid passive income option.

Chapter 13: Investing in Real Estate Without Buying Property

To bring our discussion on real estate investing to a close, let's consider the investment options that won't require you to actually own rental property. As we established in the previous chapter, one of the major downsides of owning rental property is that it ties up a significant amount of cash in just one investment. For those unable or unwilling to own, you can still benefit from the upsides of real estate through an investment vehicle known as a **REIT** (Real Estate Investment Trust), or through **Real Estate Crowdfunding**.

A REIT works in the same way as a mutual fund. Similarly to how a mutual fund maintains a portfolio of equities for their investors, a REIT maintains a portfolio of rental properties—both commercial and residential—that are leased out to tenants, and the rent that is collected is paid out to REIT investors as dividends.

In fact, REITs are required to distribute at minimum **90%** of their earnings through dividends, making it a more reliable form of passive income for investors. As long as the real estate market is doing well, investors get paid. Over the past thirty years, equity REITs have averaged a total annualized return of 10.4%, actually beating out the S&P 500, with its annualized return of 9.6%. To say the least, REITs compete with the overall stock market.

Furthermore, REITs provide for a greater degree of diversification in an investment portfolio. Real estate and equities don't move in unison, and when one is underperforming the other may balance out your overall portfolio by performing well, and vice versa.

Like companies, REITs can be publicly traded or private. Publicly-traded REITs are traded on exchanges like stocks, and must follow higher governance standards as established by the SEC, offering greater transparency to investors. You can invest in individual REITs, or invest indirectly through mutual funds and ETFs. The chief advantage of publicly-traded REITs is that they are highly liquid—though for those looking for a long-term, passive strategy, they may avail themselves by investing in a highly diversified REIT mutual fund or ETF and be done with it.

Beyond publicly-traded REITs, there are **public non-traded REITs** and **private REITs**. The former are registered with the SEC, but are not traded on an exchange. These tend to have high account minimums (such that they are out of reach for the average, individual investor), require lengthy holding times and are hence relatively illiquid, and are less transparent than publicly-traded REITs. Private REITs are even less regulated and more risky, typically available only to accredited investors.

In general, REITs offer an array of options for various types of investors, including those looking to simply diversify their portfolio and benefit from the long-term growth that real estate has historically exhibited. For those looking to have a little more skin in the game, there is the alternative of *crowdfunding*.

We've discussed crowdfunding already with regards to equity crowdfunding. Real estate crowdfunding works much the same way, with individuals or institutions raising capital from a pool of investors to then purchase real estate. Unless you are an accredited investor, you generally will not have the opportunity to pick and choose individual properties through crowdfunding. Instead, there are crowdfunding platforms—such as Fundrise, DiversyFund, Rich Uncles, RealtyMogul—that are open to non-accredited investors with account minimums as low as $500, which offer you a diversified portfolio of real estate properties.

Crowdfunding is generally higher risk than investing in a REIT, but, of course, with higher risk comes higher potential reward.

The real estate market, despite a number of short-term dips, has proven itself to be highly attractive for potential investors. Whether you are looking to develop rental income or simply to diversify your portfolio without taking on the burden of owning property, real estate offers something for anyone who is serious about their investments and long-term wealth. To put it simply, no portfolio would be complete without investment in real estate.

Section 5: Tying It All Together

Chapter 14: What now? Where do we go from here?

Over the last several chapters, you have been exposed to a deluge of passive income strategies. Now is a good time to take stock of the various means of earning alternative income that we have covered, and to consider where to go from here. We'll finish with a chapter on the "other" passive income ideas and strategies that don't quite fit into any one of the major categories (investment, online, and real estate income).

So, what have we learned?

We began with the example of the magic penny. We saw that as a result of the **power of compounding**, a doubling penny can be worth more than a million dollars. But the power of compounding is not a mere mathematical phenomenon with no application to the real world:

In the real world, our magic penny is the stock market.

The stock market, with its relatively modest 8% long-term annual return, suffices in terms of enabling your investments to grow exponentially over time. Simply by investing just $1 per day in the stock market, you can expect your money to grow to about $43,000 over the course of thirty years, setting yourself up for a better retirement than a majority of Americans. Furthermore, we established that with a time horizon of thirty years, you would have to invest roughly seven hundred dollars per month in order to become a millionaire.

There are many different ways to achieve this monthly figure, all of which can be categorized in one of two methods: **save more**, or **earn more**. Saving more of your primary income towards retirement is a noble endeavor, but often one that is not sustained. Why? Most folks approach taking control of their finances as they would taking control of their weight and figure: taking on an all-or-nothing approach in the hope of quick results, then experiencing fatigue while struggling to sustain the drastic change, and eventually reverting back to their former ways.

Now, once and for all, it's time to break this fruitless cycle that we repeatedly find ourselves in. We are self-aware, and we're smart enough to know what we can and cannot sustainably do. And so, we realize that it is pointless to attempt to save more than our **optimal savings rate**, the rate at which our savings are maximized, but not at the expense of our life satisfaction (recall the following graph).

DIMINISHING RETURNS WHEN SAVING

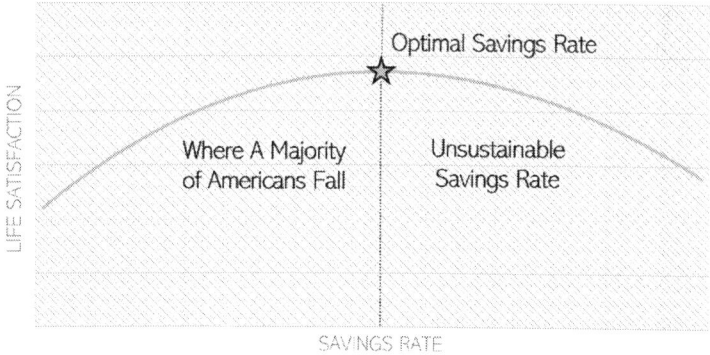

To determine our optimal savings rate, we must first take stock of our finances and determine our **current savings rate**, which can be calculated by determining how much we've spent on average over the past six months. From there, we take a **piecemeal approach** to establish our optimal savings rate, incrementally raising how much we save every month until we reach a point in which we cannot cut back any further without depriving ourselves of something that we cannot do without. Once we've determined our optimal savings rate, we **automate our savings** by setting up automatic transfers into a deposit account, so that we continue saving at our optimal savings rate moving forward.

Our optimal savings rate may fall below our **target savings rate**—the amount we *should* be saving to reach our financial goals, retirement, etc.—and that's OK. In fact, for most of us, our optimal savings rate will fall below our target savings rate. And so how do we bridge the gap? The answer, of course, lies in passive—or, more generally, alternative—income, which we divided into three major categories: investment income, online income, and real estate income.

When it comes to **investment income** and the stock market, we learned that it pays to be passive: a majority of mutual fund managers fail to beat the market, and so why put your money with them and incur high management fees, when you could be investing in a low-cost index fund that matches overall market performance? For most people with a long-term mindset, the latter is usually preferable.

We discussed **robo investing** as a passive investment income method and alternative to a traditional investment account, in which automated investing services are put to work, cutting down on management fees and making it easy to manage your money. What's more, most portfolios are built to match the market, making them ideal for long-term investment horizons. If you are looking to invest your money without tying it up into a retirement account—in cases where you have shorter-term investment goals, such as saving up for a house or college tuition—robo investing may help you reach your financial goals.

From there we proceeded to not-so-passive investment income strategies, including **value investing** (AKA the Warren Buffet approach), **momentum investing** (AKA riding the wave), **growth investing** (what's the next big thing?), and ways to invest in private companies, namely **peer-to-peer (P2P) lending** and **equity crowdfunding**. The former has to do with investing in a privately held company in the form of *debt* (you lend the company money), while the latter in the form of *equity* (you buy a stake in the company). There are countless online platforms that connect investors with businesses seeking capital in the form of debt and equity. We must bear in mind that actively managing our investments comes with no promise of greater reward, and in certain cases—such as investing in private companies—we must take on greater risk.

From investment income we moved on to the second major category of alternative income: **online income**. We learned that there are two types of online income: **digital-product income** and **physical-product Income**. Our focus was on the former, as this aligned most with alternative income that is more passive in nature. We discussed the **Digital Products Business Model** (or DPBM), which drives revenue within our *digital store*, and has three key features:

THE 3 KEY FEATURES OF THE DPBM
A **core product**, such as a book or an online course, that generates the most revenue for you, the digital store owner
One or more **complimentary products**, each of which drives traffic to the core product, and vice versa, and that are ideally monetized
A **mailing list**, or group of subscribers and followers, to which to promote new content

The common types of products we find in digital stores include: eBooks (plus Audiobooks and paperbacks), online courses, blogs, YouTube channels, and podcasts. A high revenue generating store contains multiple products, each of which is monetized and points to and promotes the other products in the digital store.

We went on to discuss physical products, or **e-commerce**, and compared the various e-commerce business models, which include (in rough order of increasing complexity): **wholesaling, dropshipping**, **print-on-demand**, and **private labeling** through Amazon FBA. The first three rely on your own website to drive revenue, while private labeling through Amazon FBA leverages Amazon's existing e-commerce store, exposing you to a greater customer base. Running an e-commerce store is hardly passive, but can be at times; establishing a customer base, expanding your business, and maintaining a competitive advantage in the market, however, will usually require you to be actively involved in the business.

From there we proceeded to the third major type of passive income, **real estate income**. We uncovered the various challenges of landlordship, including bad tenants, unforeseen expenses, and vacant units. We compared buying a rental property with cash versus financing, and found that when considering just one property, paying for it outright will lead to higher cash flow, while financing it to a higher ROI. Therefore, by financing multiple properties, we stand to make more money through a combination of rental income and appreciation.

We dove deeper into the nuances of running a rental business, some of the highlights being: a **quality rental listing** will attract quality tenants; **depreciation** is one of the best tax advantages available to landlords; research the **quantitative factors** (average rent, vacancy rate, property taxes) and the **qualitative factors** (quality of local schools, crime, local amenities, the local job market, etc.) that influence a rental market before buying; know the **landlord-tenant laws** in your state and city to avoid potential legal burdens.

Finally, we saw that you don't have to own property to invest in real estate. For those unable or unwilling to own, you can still benefit from the upsides of real estate investing through **REITs** (Real Estate Investment Trusts) or **Real Estate Crowdfunding**. REITs offer an array of options for different kinds of investors, including those looking to simply diversify their portfolio and benefit from the long-term growth that real estate has historically exhibited. Crowdfunding, on the other hand, pools together capital from individual investors to purchase real estate. Though traditionally limited to accredited investors and institutions, real estate crowdfunding has been made available to non-accredited investors thanks to online platforms such as DiversyFund and Rich Uncles that offer account minimums of $500.

Clearly, we have covered an incredible amount of alternative income strategies over the course of this book. At this point, you may be at a loss as to which ones to pursue. To help you out, I've created a handy cheat sheet that summarizes the pros and cons of all the income streams and ideas presented in this book. You can use this cheat sheet as a "quick and dirty" summary of everything we've covered, as well as a guide to help you compare different income streams and decide which ones are right for you. You can get the **Passive Income Millionaire Cheat Sheet** right now by signing up on my website:

https://districthousepublishing.com/passive

Be on the lookout for more freebies, as well as the Passive Income Millionaire *online course*, coming soon to a personal device near you.

My hope is that this book has provided you a solid framework for taking control of your finances. We live in an unprecedented period of history, marked by unlimited interconnectivity and diminishing barriers to entry. The opportunities available to us are many times greater than those of previous generations. No longer are we necessarily bound to traditional means of income, or the need to continuously save in order to secure a decent retirement.

As we established in the very beginning of this book, we are all different, and the financial habits of one individual may not be suitable for others. It is pointless to force yourself to be more frugal than what can be sustainably maintained. Fortunately, you don't have to. By determining the maximum amount of money that you can comfortably save and then automating your savings, you can free yourself from the stresses of spending too much or saving too little. From there, you can bridge any gap that exists between you and your financial goals by developing one or more passive income streams.

To help you in this quest, we'll conclude with the "other" passive income ideas and strategies that you can employ in your journey towards financial freedom.

Chapter 15: Refinancing, Airbnb, Vehicle Advertising, and Other Passive Income Ideas to Get You Started

You can scour the web for more alternative income ideas that aren't mentioned in this book. Some of these, you'll find, are less realistic than others (who wants to sign up for paid clinical trials?). So, to help you get started, I've listed below my top five most *realistic* ways to start earning passive that don't fall into the big categories of investment, online, or real estate income.

Other Passive Income Strategy #1: Refinance your loans

At the time of the publication of this book, interest rates are at an all-time low. Refinancing your loans is a kind of reverse passive income strategy: you're not necessarily earning more money, but spending less on your existing loan payments. Consider whether now is a good time to refinance your student loan, car loan, and/or mortgage. Doing so may save you a considerable sum each month, which you can think of as extra income that you can save or invest towards your financial goals.

Other Passive Income Strategy #2: Rent out your space on Airbnb

Some homeowners are willing to sublease a portion of their home, such as a basement or an extra room, to tenants. For many, this would not be worth the inconvenience. Instead, you may be willing to temporarily rent out a room or your entire space at certain times of the year. Becoming an Airbnb host comes with its own set of challenges, but these are relatively straightforward and can be easily managed.

As we learned with renting out to tenants, your **listing** is everything. A high-quality listing, with numerous, quality images and detailed descriptions will set your place apart from the competition. Research similar Airbnb listings in your area to get a sense for the market and how much you can expect to make. If you are willing to open up your home to guests, this can be a great and reliable alternative income stream.

Other Passive Income Strategy #3: Rent out storage space, parking space, your car, and/or personal items

Airbnb's business model has been taken and copied across a plethora of product offerings. You hear "Turo is the Airbnb for cars", "Neighbor is the Airbnb for storage space", and so on. You can rent out practically anything these days, from an extra parking spot to your car itself. Consider whether you have extra storage space around the house, a parking space, a car, or personal items—such as electronics, musical instruments, bikes/electric scooters, etc.—that people would be interested in renting. There are numerous websites and apps out there for each of these categories; consider posting on multiple to increase the odds of obtaining customers. For car sharing there is Turo, Getaround, HyreCar; for storage space there is Neighbor, StoreAtMyHouse; for personal items there is Fat Llama, BabyQuip—of course, one should not fail to consider the traditional routes of Craigslist and Facebook as potential platforms for your listings.

Other Passive Income Strategy #4: Advertise on your car

Also known as "wrapping," advertising on your vehicle is an easy way to earn extra cash every month—upwards of a few hundred dollars per month—assuming you are comfortable with it. Beware of scammers, however, as they are common in this market. Legitimate car wrapping companies that you may want to consider include Carvertise, Wrapify, and Nickelytics.

Other Passive Income Strategy #5: Start a coin-operated machine business

Admittedly, this alternative income idea can be a bit more involved than the previous ones. Still, getting started with a vending machine business is not too difficult. Startup costs are low, and the vending machine itself (or other coin-operated machines, such as arcade games) can be financed. Furthermore, you have the option to establish business contacts on your own or buy an existing vending machine business whose customers you will acquire. Once you've set up machines at various business locations, running the business is simply a matter of restocking, collecting money, and occasional maintenance.

There you have it. I want to thank you for coming along on this journey with me, and I hope this book proves useful in advancing you towards your financial goals. Be sure to visit my website, where you can sign up to get the Passive Income Millionaire Cheat Sheet and receive updates on new materials and content as they're released. Every year there are new opportunities and platforms for earning passive income, so be sure to sign up and stay in the know. So long for now, and best of luck in your passive income pursuits!

Printed in Great Britain
by Amazon

29368636R00052